Dog Food
Recipes
Cookbook

Karen L. Armstrong

Binghamton, New York, USA

i

Acknowledgements

I'm totally inspired by Pet Comfort Products!

www.Pet-Comfort-Products.com

Contents

Jake's Dog Biscuits
Lab Liver-Chip Cookie
Labrador Loaf
Lhasa Apso Lamb
Liver Brownies
Liver Treats
Liver Treats For Dogs
Lucy's Liver Slivers
Massive Mastiff Munchy Muffins
Meat and Grain Menu
Meatball Mania
Munchie Crunchy Meat Treats
MuttLoaf
Mutt's favorite rice n' hamburger
Muttzoh Balls
Peanut Butter and Honey Dog Biscuits
Peanut Butter Cookies
Peanut Butter Dog Biscuits
Peanut Butter & Oats Glazed Goodies
Pet Party Mix
Pet Puffs
Pooch Peanut Butter Swirls
Poochie Pint-Sized Carrot Treats
Poodle Pasta
Potatoes Au Canine
Pumpkin-Patch Dog Biscuits
Puppy Formulas

Ravioli Woofer Stuffing
Rice Flour Dog Cookie

Ace's Favorite Cheesy Dog Biscuits

1 1/2 cups whole wheat flour
1 1/4 cups grated cheddar cheese
1/4 pound margarine -- corn oil
1 clove garlic -- crushed
1 pinch salt
1/4 cup Milk -- or as needed

Grate the cheese into a bowl and let stand until it reaches room temperature. Cream the cheese with the softened margarine, garlic, salt and flour. Add enough milk to form into a ball.

Chill for 1/2 hour. Roll onto floured board. Cut into shapes and bake at 375 degrees for 15 minutes or until slightly brown, and firm.

Makes 2 to 3 dozen, depending on size.

Alfalfa Hearts

2 cups whole wheat flour
1/2 cup soy flour
1 teaspoon bone meal -- optional
2 tablespoons nutritional yeast
1 tablespoon lecithin -- optional
1/2 teaspoon salt
1/4 teaspoon garlic powder
3 tablespoons alfalfa sprouts -- chopped
1 cup brown rice -- cooked
3 tablespoons canola oil
1/2 cup water

Combine flours, bone meal, yeast, lecithin, salt, garlic powder and alfalfa leaves. Add rice and oil. Combine well. Add
1/4 cup water and mix well. Dough should be very easy to
handle, not crumbly. Add more water if needed to achieve
proper consistency.

Lightly flour board or counter and roll out dough to 1/4 inch
thickness. Cut with 2 1/2 inch cutter. Bake at 350 degrees
for 25 minutes.

Makes 3 dozen.

Alfie And Archie's Dog Biscuits

2 1/2 cups whole wheat flour
1/2 cup dry milk -- powder
1/2 teaspoon salt
1/2 teaspoon garlic powder
1 teaspoon brown sugar
6 tablespoons beef fat
1 egg -- beaten
1/2 cup ice water

1. Preheat oven to 350. Lightly oil a cookie sheet. Combine flour, dry milk, salt, garlic powder and sugar. Cut in meat drippings until mixture resembles corn meal. Mix in egg. Add enough water so that mixture forms a ball. Using your fingers, pat out dough onto cookie sheet to half inch thick. Cut with cookie cutter or knife and remove scraps. Scraps can be formed again and baked.

2. Bake 25-30 minutes. Remove from tray and cool on rack.

An Apple a Day Dog Treat

2 cups whole wheat flour
1/2 cup unbleached flour
1/2 cup cornmeal
1 apple -- chopped or grated
1 egg -- beaten
1/3 cup vegetable oil
1 tablespoon brown sugar, packed
3/8 cup water

Preheat oven to 350 degrees. Spray cookie sheet with vegetable oil spray. Lightly dust work surface with flour. Blend
flours and cornmeal m large mixing bowl. Add apple, egg,
oil, brown sugar and water; mix until well blended.

On floured surface, roll dough out to 7/8-inch thickness. Cut
with cookie cutters of desired shape and size. Place treats on
prepared sheet.

Bake in preheated oven 35 to 40 minutes. Turn off oven.
Leave door closed 1 hour to crisp treats. Remove treats from
oven.
Store baked treats in airtight container or plastic bag and
place in refrigerator or freezer.

MAKES 2 to 2 1/2 dozen

Apple Cinnamon Doggie Biscuits

1 package apple, dried
1 teaspoon Cinnamon -- (I usually just shake some in)
1 Tablespoon parsley, freeze-dried
1 Tablespoon Garlic Powder
1 cup ice water
1/2 cup Corn Oil
5 cups flour
1/2 cup powdered milk
2 large eggs
1 tablespoon corn oil

Put the apples in a food processor so that pieces are small. Combine in a bowl all of the ingredients -- can add oil or water if dough is too dry. Using a rolling pin roll out dough to about 3/16" thick (can make thinner or thicker). Using a cookie cutter -- cut into shapes -- place on cookie sheets. Bake at 350 degrees for approx 20 -25 minutes (until golden).

NOTE: if you substitute corn meal just subtract about 3/4 cup from flour and add Corn meal

Apple Crunch Pupcakes

2 3/4 cups water
1/4 cup unsweetened applesauce
2 tablespoons honey
1 medium egg
1/8 teaspoon vanilla extract
4 cups whole wheat flour
1 cup apple, dried
1 tablespoon baking powder

Preheat oven to 350 degrees. In a small bowl, mix together water, applesauce, honey, egg, and vanilla. In a large bowl, combine flour, apple chips, and baking powder. Add liquid ingredients to dry ingredients and mix until very well blended. Pour into greased muffin pans, Bake 1 1/4 hours, or until a toothpick inserted in the center comes out dry. Store in a sealed container.

Makes 12 to 14 pupcakes

Aunt Bianca's Dog Biscuits

2 1/2 cups whole wheat flour
1/2 cup nonfat dry milk powder
1 teaspoon garlic powder
1 egg -- beaten

Flavoring: Meat drippings, broth or water from canned tuna (enough to make a stiff dough).

Combine flour, powdered milk and garlic powder in a medium sized bowl. Add beaten egg, flavoring and mix well with hands. Dough should be very stiff. If necessary add more flavoring.

On a well floured surface, roll out dough to 1/4 inch thickness. Cut with shaped cookie cutters of your choice.

Place biscuits on cookie sheets and bake at 350 degrees for 30 minutes.

Baby Food Doggie Cookies

3 jars baby food, meat, beef, strained -- *see Note
1/4 cup cream of wheat -- *see Note
1/4 cup dry milk

Combine ingredients in bowl and mix well. Roll into small balls and place on well-greased cookie sheet. Flatten slightly with a fork. Bake in preheated 350 degree oven for 15 min. until brown.

Cool on wire racks and STORE IN REFRIGERATOR. Also freezes well.

NOTE: Carrot, Chicken or Beef baby food. substituting wheat germ for cream of wheat.

Bacon Bites

3 cups whole wheat flour
1/2 cup milk
1 egg
1/4 cup bacon grease -- or vegetable oil
1 teaspoon garlic powder
4 slices bacon -- crumbled
1/2 cup cold water

Mix ingredients together thoroughly. Roll out on a floured surface to 1/2 - 1/4" thickness. Bake for 35-40 minutes in a 325 degree oven.

Bacon Bits for Dogs

6 slices cooked bacon -- crumbled
4 eggs -- well beaten
1/8 cup bacon grease
1 cup water
1/2 cup powdered milk -- non-fat
2 cup graham flour
2 cup wheat germ
1/2 cup cornmeal

Mix ingredients with a strong spoon; drop heaping table-spoonfuls onto a greased baking sheet. Bake in a 350 oven for 15 minutes. Turn off oven and leave cookies on baking sheet in the oven overnight to dry out.

Baker's Bagels

1 cup whole wheat flour
1 cup unbleached flour
1 package yeast -- 1/4 ounce
1 cup chicken broth -- warmed
1 tablespoon honey

1. Preheat oven to 375°.

2. In large bowl combine the whole wheat flour with the yeast. Add 2/3 cup chicken broth and honey and beat for about 3 minutes. Gradually add the remaining flour. Knead the dough for a few minutes until smooth and moist, but not wet (use reserve broth as necessary).

3. Cover the dough and let it rest for about 5 minutes. Divide the dough into about 15-20 pieces, rolling each piece into a smooth ball. Punch a hole into each ball with your finger or end of spoon and gently pull the dough so the hole is about an 1/2" wide. Don't be too fussy here, the little bagels rise into shape when they bake.

4. Place all the bagels on a greased cookie sheet and allow to rise 5 minutes. Bake for 25 minutes. Turn the heat off and allow the bagels to cool in the oven.

BARF Breakfast (med size dog)

1/4 cup rolled oats
1/2 cup yogurt
1/4 cup vegetables -- *see Note
250 mgs vitamin C -- for dogs. Crushed
1 teaspoon honey
1 teaspoon apple cider vinegar
1 teaspoon kelp seaweed powder -- *see Note
1 teaspoon alfalfa powder -- *see Note
1 digestive enzyme -- for dogs Optional
1 teaspoon flax seed oil -- *see Note
1/4 cup kibble -- optional

Soak rolled oats in yogurt overnight. Mix all ingredients and serve. Add kibble if desired.

Note: shredded, lightly steamed or pureed. carrots, celery, spinach, yams and/or broccoli, apples etc.

Note: items can be purchased at health food store or pet store.

BARF Dinner (med size dog)

3/4 pound Raw Meat -- *see Note
1 egg -- raw
1/2 clove garlic -- chopped
2 tablespoons yogurt
1 teaspoon honey
1 tablespoon apple cider vinegar
1/2 teaspoon flax seed oil -- *see Note
1 teaspoon kelp seaweed powder -- *see Note
1 teaspoon alfalfa powder -- *see Note
250 mgs vitamin C -- for dogs
1/4 cup kibble -- optional

Mix together and serve.

*Note: raw beef chunks (not ground), raw chicken, mackerel, or lamb etc. twice a week use liver or kidney.

Note: found in health food store or pet store

Barking Barley Brownies

1 1/4 pounds beef liver -- or chicken liver
2 cups wheat germ
2 tablespoons whole wheat flour
1 cup cooked barley
2 whole eggs
3 tablespoons peanut butter
1 clove garlic
1 tablespoon olive oil
1 teaspoon salt -- optional

Pre heat oven to 350.

Liquefy liver and garlic clove in a blender, when its smooth add eggs and peanut butter. Blend till smooth.

In separate mixing bowl combine wheat germ, whole wheat flour, and cooked Barley. Add processed liver mixture, olive oil and salt. Mix well. spread mixture in a greased 9x9 baking dish. Bake for 20 minutes or till done.

When cool cut into pieces that accommodate your doggies size.

Store in refrigerator or freezer.

Basenji Stew

4 small parsnip -- **see Note
2 whole yellow squash -- cubed
2 whole Sweet potatoes -- peeled and cubed
2 whole Zucchini -- cubed
5 whole tomatoes -- canned
1 can garbanzo beans, canned -- *see Note 15 oz
1/2 cup Couscous
1/4 cup Raisins
1 teaspoon Ground coriander
1/2 teaspoon Ground turmeric
1/2 teaspoon Ground cinnamon
1/2 teaspoon Ground ginger
1/4 teaspoon Ground cumin
3 cups Water -- *see Note

** Kohlrabi may be substituted for the parsnips.
* Chick-peas or 3 cups chicken stock

Combine all the ingredients in a large saucepan. Bring to a boil, lower the heat, and simmer until the vegetables are tender, about 30 minutes. Place over cook brown rice or barley

Beef and Rice Moochies

1 jar babyfood, dinner, vegetables and beef, strained
2 1/2 cups flour, all-purpose
1 cup whole wheat flour
1 cup rice
1 package unflavored gelatin
1 whole egg
2 tablespoons vegetable oil
1 cup powdered milk
1 package yeast
1/4 cup warm water
1 beef bouillon cube

Dissolve yeast in warm water. Mix dry ingredients in large bowl. Add yeast, egg, oil, baby food and dissolved beef bouillon. Mix well. Mixture will be very dry, knead with hands until it forms a ball. Roll out on floured surface to 1/4 inch thickness, cut in 1 or 2 inch circles. Bake on un-greased cookie sheet 30 minutes at 300 degrees. Store in refrigerator.

Beef Twists

3 1/2 cups flour, all-purpose
1 cup cornmeal
1 package unflavored gelatin
1/4 cup milk
1 egg
1/4 cup corn oil
1 jar Baby food, meat, beef, strained
1 beef bouillon cube
3/4 cup boiling water -- or beef stock

Dissolve bouillon cube in water. Sift dry ingredients in large bowl. Add milk, egg, oil, beef and beef bouillon. Stir until well mixed. Roll out on a floured surface to 1/4 inch thickness. Cut in 1/4 inch by 3 inch strips, twisting each stick 3 turns before placing on cookie sheet. Bake 35-40 minutes at 400 degrees. Store in refrigerator.

Birthday Cake for Pups

1 1/2 cups all-purpose flour
1 1/2 teaspoons baking powder
1/2 cup soft butter
1/2 cup corn oil
1 jar baby food, meat, beef, strained
4 eggs
2 strips beef jerky -- (2 to 3)

Preheat oven to 325 degrees. Grease and flour an 8x5x3 inch loaf pan. Cream butter until smooth. Add corn oil, baby food, and eggs. Mix until smooth. Mix dry ingredients into beef mixture until batter is smooth. Crumble beef jerky and fold into batter. Pour batter into loaf pan. Bake 1 hour and 10 minutes. cool on wire rack 15 minutes. Ice with plain yogurt or cottage cheese. Store uneaten cake in refrigerator.

Biscuits For Dogs

1 cup oatmeal -- uncooked
1/3 cup margarine
1 tablespoon beef bouillon granules
5 1/2 cups hot water
1 tablespoon garlic powder -- optional
3/4 cup powdered milk
3/4 cup cornmeal
3 cups whole wheat flour
1 whole egg -- beaten

Pour hot water over oatmeal, margarine, and bouillon; let stand for 6 min. Stir in milk, cornmeal, and egg. Add flour, 1/2 c. at a time; mix well after each addition. Knead 3 - 4 min., adding more flour it necessary to make a very STIFF dough. Roll or pat dough to 1/2" thickness. Cut into dog bone shapes with cookie cutter. Bake at 325 degrees for 50 min. on baking parchment Allow to cool and dry out until hard. Store in container.

BJ'S Peanutty Pupcicles

1 ripe banana
1/2 cup peanut butter
1/4 cup wheat germ
1/4 cup chopped peanuts

Mash banana's and peanut butter, stir in wheat germ. Chill 1 hour. Place in container, store in refrigerator or freezer.

Bone A Fidos

2 1/4 teaspoons Dry yeast
1/4 cup warm water
1 Pinch sugar
3 1/2 cups All-purpose flour
2 cups Whole wheat flour
2 cups Cracked wheat
1 cup Rye flour
1/2 cup Nonfat dry milk
4 teaspoons Kelp powder
4 cups Beef broth -- or chicken
GLAZE:1 large egg
2 tablespoons Milk

Equipment: Cookie sheets lined with parchment or aluminum foil; rolling pin; 3-31/2" bone cutter or 2 1/2" round cookie cutter.

Place 2 oven racks in the upper and lower thirds of the oven. Preheat oven to 300 degrees. Sprinkle the dry yeast or crumple the compressed yeast over the water (110 degrees if dry yeast, 100 degrees if compressed yeast). Add a pinch of sugar and allow the yeast to sit in a draft-free spot for 10 - 20 minutes. The mixture should be full of bubbles. If not, the yeast is too old to be useful.

In a large bowl, place all the dry ingredients and stir to blend them. Add the yeast mixture and 3 cups of the broth. Using your hands, in the bowl, mix to form the dough, adding more broth if needed to make the dough smooth and supple. Half a batch at a time, knead the dough briefly on a lightly floured counter. (Keep the second batch of dough covered with a moist towel while shaping and cutting the fast.)

Roll out the dough into an 18 x 13 x 1/4" rectangle. Cut it into desired shapes, using a 3 - 3 l/2-inch bone cutter or a 2 l/2-inch round cookie cutter. Re-roll the scraps. Repeat the procedure with the remaining dough.

For an attractive shine, lightly beat together the egg and milk. Brush the glaze on the cookies. Bake for 45 to 60 minutes or until brown and firm.

For even baking rotate the cookie sheets from top to bottom three quarters of the way through the baking period. Use a small, angled metal spatula or pancake turner to transfer the cookies to wire racks to cool completely.

Store in an airtight container at room temperature. The dough must be used immediately. The baked cookies will keep for many months.
Allow cookie sheets to cool completely between batches.

Bone Bonanza

1/2 pound ground beef -- uncooked
1/4 cup chicken broth
1/3 cup black beans, cooked -- mashed
1/3 cup cottage cheese
1 teaspoon soy sauce

Combine ground meat and chicken broth in a bowl. Add the black beans and cottage cheese. Add soy sauce. Mix all of the ingredients together thoroughly. Mold the mixture into bone shapes and place on a cookie sheet. Bake for 45 minutes in a 375 degree oven. Let cool.

Boo's Biscuits

3 1/2 cup whole wheat flour
2 cup Quaker oats
1 cup milk
1/2 cup hot water
2 beef or chicken bouillon cubes
1/2 cup meat drippings

Dissolve bouillon cubes in hot water. Add milk and drippings and beat.
In a separate bowl, mix flour and oatmeal. Pour liquid ingredients into dry ingredients and mix well. Press onto an ungreased cookie sheet and cut into shapes desired. Bake at 300 degrees for 1 hour. Turn off heat and leave in the oven to harden. Refrigerate after baking.

Bow Wow Biscuits

2 1/2 cups whole wheat flour
1/2 cup wheat germ
1/2 cup powdered milk
1/2 teaspoon salt
1/2 teaspoon garlic powder
8 tablespoons bacon grease -- or margarine
1 egg -- beaten
1 teaspoon brown sugar
2 tablespoons beef broth -- or chicken
1/2 cup ice water
6 slices Bacon -- crumbled, optional
1/2 cup cheddar cheese, shredded -- optional

In a big mixing bowl, mix all the ingredients thoroughly to form a dough. Roll the dough out with a rolling pin and use a cookie cutter to make shapes for cookies, Bake cookies at 350 degrees for 20 - 25 min.

Bow Wow Burritos

1 tablespoon oil
12 ounces cooked beef -- *see Note
1 clove garlic -- minced
3 tablespoons chunky peanut butter
1 can sweet potatoes -- (23-oz.) drained
1 can black beans -- (15-oz.) rinsed
1 teaspoon chili powder
1 teaspoon cumin
1/2 teaspoon cinnamon
2 teaspoons beef bouillon -- powder
6 flour tortillas -- (10-inch)
2 tablespoons cilantro -- chopped
6 tablespoons cheese -- shredded
6 tablespoons vegetables -- *see Note

Heat oil in large skillet over medium heat until hot. Add garlic; cook and stir 2 to 3 minutes or until tender. Stir in
peanut butter, sweet potatoes and beans; mash slightly. Add
cumin, cinnamon and chili powder, beef bouillon; mix well.
Reduce heat to low; add beef, cover and simmer 2 to 3 minutes or until thoroughly heated, stirring occasionally.

Meanwhile, heat tortillas according to package directions. To
serve, spoon and spread scant 1/2 cup mixture across center
third of each tortilla with one piece of meat in center.

Top each with 1 tablespoon sour cream, 1 teaspoon cilantro,
I tablespoon Cheese spread to cover mixture.

Fold sides of each tortilla 1 inch over filling. Fold bottom 1/3
of tortilla over filling; roll again to enclose filling.

*Note: Beef or chicken cut into 1/2 inch strips, or "meatless" meat for the vegetarian doggies.

*Note: Optional... Shredded veggies for added nutrition, carrots, green beans, broccoli etc.

Serving Ideas : Add 1 Teaspoon Dog Oil Supplement and 1 teaspoon Dog Powder Mix Supplement for added nutrition before folding burritos.

Bread Machine Dog Biscuits

3/4 cup Beef stock -- *see Note
1 egg
3 tablespoons oil
1 cup all-purpose flour
1 cup whole wheat flour
1/3 cup Bulgur -- *see Note
1/3 cup Bran
1/4 cup nonfat dry milk
1/4 teaspoon Garlic powder
1 1/2 teaspoons yeast

Place ingredients in bread pan according to manufacturers directions and press "Dough" cycle. When machine beeps, remove dough to lightly floured countertop and with a rolling pin, roll dough out to 1/4" thickness.

Using a dog bone cookie cutter (or any small seasonal cookie cutters), cut out dog biscuits and place on a lightly greased cookie sheet or one sprinkled with cornmeal. Re-roll scraps and repeat till all dough is used up. Place in a warm location and let rise 30 minutes. Bake at 325 for 30 minutes until brown and no longer soft. Place on a rack to cool. Store in an airtight container.

* Chicken, Vegetable Or use hot water and 2 or 3 -bouillon cubes.

** If you don't have bulgur try substituting something like a 7-grain cereal.

Breath Busters Biscuits

1 1/2 cups whole wheat flour
1 1/2 cups Bisquick ® baking mix
1/2 cup mint leaves -- loosely packed
1/4 cup milk
4 tablespoons margarine1 egg
1 1/2 tablespoons maple syrup -- or corn syrup

Combine all ingredients in food processor, process until well mixed, mint is chopped, and a large ball forms. Press or roll on non-stick surface (floured board or ceramic) to a thickness of 1/4-1/2". Cut into 1x2" strips or with bone-shaped cookie cutter and place on non-stick cookie pan. Bake at 375° for 20 minutes or until lightly browned.
Cool and store in air-tight container. Makes about 30 medium biscuits.

Buddy Boys Dog Biscuits

1 cup whole wheat flour
1/2 cup all-purpose flour
3/4 cup nonfat dry milk powder
1/2 cup oats, rolled (raw) -- quick cooking
1/2 cup yellow cornmeal
1 teaspoon sugar

Cut in 1/3 cup shortening until mix is coarse crumbs. Stir in 1 egg. Dissolve 1 tablespoon instant chicken or beef bouillon granules in 1/2 cup water. Stir liquid into flour mix with a fork. Form dough into a ball and knead on floured board for 5 minutes. Divide ball in half and roll each portion until 1/2 inch thick. Use a cookie cutter or shape biscuits. Put 6 on a plate and microwave at medium for 5 to 10 minutes or until firm and dry to touch. Turn biscuits over after 1/2 cooking time

Bulldog Banana Bites

2 1/4 cups whole wheat flour
1/2 cup powdered milk -- nonfat
1 egg
1/3 cup banana -- ripe, mashed
1/4 cup vegetable oil
1 beef bouillon cube
1/2 cup water -- hot
1 tablespoon brown sugar

Mix all ingredients until will blended. Knead for 2 minutes on a floured surface. Roll to 1/4 " thickness. Use a 2 1/2" bone shaped cookie cutter (or any one you prefer). Bake for 30 minutes in a 300 degrees oven on ungreased cookie pans.

Bulldog Brownies

1/2 cup shortening
3 tablespoons honey
4 eggs
1 teaspoon vanilla
1 cup whole wheat flour
1/4 cup carob flour
1/2 teaspoon baking powder

Frosting
12 ounces nonfat cream cheese
2 teaspoons honey

Cream shortening and honey together thoroughly. Add remaining ingredients. Beat well. Bake in a greased cookie sheet (10x15") for 25 minutes at 350 degrees. Cool completely.

FROSTING: Blend together. Spread frosting over cool brownies. Cut into 3 inch or 1 1/2 inch squares

Canine Carrot Cookies

2 cups carrots -- boiled and pureed
2 eggs
2 tablespoons garlic -- minced
2 cups unbleached flour -- *see Note
1 cup rolled oats
1/4 cup wheat germ
*or rice flour or rye flour.

Combine carrots, eggs and garlic. Mix until smooth. Add dry ingredients. Roll out on heavily floured surface and cut into bars or desired shapes. Bake at 300 degrees for 45 minutes or to desired crunchiness. The centers will continue to harden as they cool. Brush with egg white before baking for a glossy finish.

Canine Cookies #1

1 1/2 cups whole wheat flour
1 cup all-purpose flour
1 cup powdered milk -- non-fat
1/3 cup bacon grease -- *see Note
1 egg -- lightly beaten
1 cup cold water

In a bowl, combine flour and milk powder. Drizzle with melted fat. Add egg and water; mix well. Gather dough into a ball. On floured surface, pat out dough. Roll out to 1/2 inch thickness. Cut into desired shapes. Gather up scraps of dough and repeat rolling and cutting. Bake on ungreased baking sheets in 350 degree oven for 50 - 60 minutes or until crispy.

Note: Beef fat or Chicken fat can be used

Makes about 36 - 2 1/2 inch biscuits. Store in the fridge.

Canine Cookies #2

1/2 cup nonfat dry milk
1 egg -- well beaten
1 1/4 cups all-purpose flour
1 1/4 cups wheat flour
1/2 teaspoon garlic powder
1/2 teaspoon onion salt
1 1/2 teaspoons brown sugar
1/2 cup water
6 tablespoons gravy
2 jars baby food, meat, beef, strained

Combine ingredients and shape into ball. Roll out on floured board, Use extra flour if needed. Cut with knife or cookie cutter. Bake at 350 degrees for 25 to 30 min. Cool. Should be quite hard.

Canine Meat and Grain Menu

2 cups cooked brown rice
2/3 cup Lean beef
2 teaspoons lard -- or veggie oil
1/4 cup vegetables -- no onion*
Supplements

Mix the above. You can cook the meat if you want to, use your judgment. Serve slightly warm.*For supplements, add 2 tsp. powder and 1 tsp. oil to feed daily- now this is for a 5-15 lb. dog

Carob Cornered Crunchies

2 1/4 cups whole wheat flour
1 egg
1/4 cup applesauce
1/4 cup vegetable oil
1 beef bouillon -- or chicken
1/2 cup hot water1 tablespoon honey
1 tablespoon molasses
1 cup carob bar -- about

Mix all ingredients together until well blended. Knead dough two minutes on a lightly floured surface. Roll to 1/4" thickness. Bake on an ungreased cookie sheet for 30 minutes in a 300 degree oven. Cool.
Melt carob chips in microwave or saucepan. Dip cool biscuits in carob or lay on a flat surface and brush carob over the biscuits with a pastry brush. Let cool.

Champion Cheese & Veggies Chews

1/2 cup grated cheese -- room temp.
3 tablespoons vegetable oil
3 teaspoons applesauce
1/2 cup vegetables -- what ever you like
1 clove garlic -- crushed
1 cup whole wheat flour
nonfat milk

Mix cheese, oil and applesauce together. Add veggies, garlic, and flour. Combine thoroughly. Add just enough milk to help form a ball. Cover and chill for one hour. Roll onto a floured surface and cut into shapes. Bake in a preheated 375 degree oven for 15 minutes or until golden brown. Let cool.

Cheese and Bacon Dog Biscuits

3/4 cup Flour
1/2 teaspoon Baking Soda
1/2 teaspoon Salt
2/3 cup Butter
2/3 cup Brown Sugar
1 Egg
1 teaspoon Vanilla extract
1 1/2 cups oatmeal
1 cup Cheddar Cheese -- shredded
1/2 cup Wheat Germ
1/2 pound Bacon -- or bacon bits

Combine flour, soda and salt; mix well and set aside. Cream butter and sugar, beat in egg and vanilla. Add flour mix mixing well. Stir in oats, cheese, wheat germ and bacon. Drop by rounded tablespoon onto ungreased baking sheets. Bake at 350 for 16 minutes. Cool and let the critters enjoy!

Cheese And Garlic Dog Cookies

1 1/2 cups whole wheat flour
1 1/4 cups cheddar cheese -- grated
1/4 pound margarine -- corn oil
1 clove garlic -- crushed
1 Pinch salt

Cream the cheese with the softened margarine, garlic, salt, and flour. Add enough milk to form into a ball. Chill for 1/2 hour. Roll onto floured board. Cut into shapes and bake at 375 for 15 minutes or until slightly brown, and firm.

MAKES 2 to 3 dozen, depending on size.

Cheese N Garlic Bites

1 cup wheat flour
1 cup cheddar cheese -- grated
1 tablespoon garlic powder
1 tablespoon butter -- softened
1/2 cup milk

Mix flour and cheese together. Add garlic powder and softened butter. Slowly add milk till you form a stiff dough. You may not need all of the milk. Knead on floured board for a few minutes. Roll out to 1/4 inch thickness. Cut into shapes and place on ungreased cookie sheet. Bake 350 degrees oven for 15 minutes. Let cool in oven with the door slightly open until cold and firm. Refrigerate to keep fresh.

Cheesey Dog Cookies

2 cups All-Purpose flour -- un-sifted
1 1/4 cups cheddar cheese -- shredded
2 cloves Garlic -- finely chopped
1/2 cup Vegetable oil
4 tablespoons Water -- (4 to 5)

Combine everything except water. Whisk in food processor until consistency of cornmeal. Then add water until mixture forms a ball. Roll it into 1/2" thickness and cut into shapes. Bake on ungreased cookie sheets about 10 min. (depending on size of shapes) at 400. Cool and store in refrigerator.

Cheesy Carrot Muffins

1 cup all-purpose flour
1 cup whole wheat flour
1 tablespoon baking powder
1 cup cheddar cheese -- Shredded
1 cup carrot -- grated
2 large eggs
1 cup milk

Preheat oven to 350 degrees. Grease a muffin tin or line it with paper baking cups. Combine the flours and baking powder and mix well. Add the cheese and carrots and use your fingers to mix them into the flour until they are well-distributed. In another bowl, beat the eggs. Then whisk in the milk and vegetable oil. Pour this over the flour mixture and stir gently until just combined. Fill the muffin cups three-quarters full with the mixture. Bake for 20-25 minutes or until the muffins feel springy. Be sure to let the muffins cool before letting your dog do any taste testing! One muffin for medium to large dog, half a muffin for a toy or small dog.

Chewy Cheesy Chihuahua Pizza

Crust

2 cups cake flour
1 1/4 cups whole wheat flour
1/4 cup olive oil
1 egg
1 cup water
1 teaspoon baking soda

Sauce & Toppings

1 tomato
1 cup tomato puree
1 clove garlic
1/4 cup parmesan cheese -- grated
1/2 teaspoon oregano
1/2 teaspoon basil
2/3 cup cooked rice

CRUST: Mix all ingredients together. Knead on a lightly floured surface. Spray a regular sized, 12 " pizza pan with nonstick spray. Next, spread the dough to the edges of the pan, forming a lip around the ends. Set aside.

Sauce & Toppings: In a food processor, blend tomato, tomato puree and garlic. Spoon the mixture over the pizza crust. Sprinkle the cheese and spices evenly over sauce. Cut the pizza into slices with a pizza cutter or sharp knife.

Bake in a 325 degree oven for 25 minutes. Take out and sprinkle rice evenly over pizza. Return to oven and bake 25 minutes more. Yield: one 12 inch pizza.

Chicken Flavored Dog Biscuits

2 1/2 teaspoons dry yeast
1/4 cup warm water
1 teaspoon salt -- optional
1 egg
1 cup chicken broth -- slightly warmed
1 cup whole wheat flour
1/2 cup rye flour -- optional
1/2 cup cornmeal
1 cup cracked wheat
1 1/2 cups all-purpose flour

In a large bowl, dissolve yeast in warm water. Add salt, one beaten egg, and the warmed chicken broth. Add all flour except the all-purpose flour and mix well. Slowly add all-purpose flour until a stiff dough is formed and it can be kneaded by hand. Knead for only a couple minutes, just enough to get the dough to hold together. Roll out dough about 1/4" thick and cut with cookie cutters, Place biscuits on a large cookie tray and place directly in a 300 degree oven, they don't need to rise. Bake for 45 min. and then turn off the oven. You can let them sit in the oven overnight and in the morning they will be real hard and good for your dog's teeth. You could also vary this recipe by adding milk for a milk-bone type biscuit or shortening for a little extra fat. Try different liquids and even honey or molasses, Check with your veterinarian for any other nutritional suggestions.

Chicken Garlic Birthday Cake

1 chicken bouillon cube
1 cup Whole-wheat flour
2 cups Wheat germ
1/2 cup Cornmeal
2 Eggs
1/2 cup Vegetable oil
1 tablespoon Minced garlic
2 cups water
vegetable oil spray -- Garlic Flavor

Preheat oven to 375 degrees. Dissolve bouillon cube in warm water. Combine flour, wheat germ, cornmeal, eggs, oil, garlic and water. Spray two cake pans with garlic-flavored oil, and sprinkle with flour. Bake 50 minutes. After removing cake from oven, turn upside down and let cool.

MAKES two small cakes

Chow Chow Chicken

2 chicken thighs -- or white meat
1 stalk celery -- sliced thick
3 carrot -- peeled and halved
2 small potato -- peeled and cubed
2 cups rice -- uncooked

Place chicken pieces in large pot. Cover with cold water (5 -6 cups). Add carrots, celery, and potatoes to water. Add salt to taste if you want. Cover and simmer on low heat about 2 hours until the chicken becomes tender. Add the rice, cover and cook over low heat for about 30 minutes until the rice is tender and most of the liquid is absorbed. Remove soup from heat. Pull the chicken meat off the bone (if will practically fall off), discard bones. Return shredded pieces to pot. Stir well. Let cool. Store in the refrigerator or freeze.

Chow Chow Stew

1 tablespoon olive oil
2 pounds beef -- *see Note
2 cups cabbage -- chopped
3 cloves garlic -- minced, up to 4
18 ounces canned sweet potatoes -- drained and chopped
14 1/2 ounces canned tomato wedges -- undrained
1 1/2 cups tomato juice
3/4 cup apple juice1 teaspoon ginger root -- up to 2, grated
2 cups green beans, frozen -- cut crosswise
1/3 cup peanut butter
6 cups cooked brown rice

Heat the oil in a large skillet over medium-high heat. Cook Beef, Add the cabbage and garlic; cook, stirring, until the cabbage is tender-crisp, about 5 minutes. Stir in the sweet potatoes, tomatoes, tomato juice, apple juice, ginger. Reduce the heat to medium-low; cover. Simmer until hot and bubbling, about 6 minutes. Stir in the green beans and simmer, uncovered, for 5 minutes. Stir in the peanut butter until well-blended and hot, about 1 minute. Spoon over rice.

*Note: Low Fat, or use chicken, lamb, fish. Liver can be used as well.

Classic Canine Cookies

4 cups whole wheat flour
1/4 cup cornmeal
1/4 cup cooked rice
1 egg
2 tablespoons vegetable oil
Juice from a small orange
1 2/3 cups water

Mix all ingredients together well. Turn out onto a lightly floured surface and knead. Roll out dough to about 1/8 inch thickness and cut out desired shapes... doggy bones, paws, balls, etc.

Dipping Sauce:

#1
3 cups vanilla chips
1 Tbsp. spinach powder
1 tsp. garlic powder
1 tsp. vegetable oil

#2
3 cups carob chips
1 tsp. vegetable oil
1 tsp. turmeric powder

Melt chips in a double boiler or microwave. Add oils and seasonings. Dip tips of cookies, when cooled, into desired sauce and place on a pan lined with wax paper until set.

Corgi Crumpets

2 1/2 cups cornmeal
1 1/2 cups cake flour
2 tablespoons vegetable oil
1 egg
2/3 cup honey
1/2 teaspoon baking powder
1/2 teaspoon cinnamon
1/2 teaspoon nutmeg
1 small apple
1 1/3 cups water
1/2 cup rolled oats

Preheat oven to 350. In a bowl, mix all ingredients except the apple and rolled oats. Grate apple into mixture. With an ice cream scoop, fill into muffin pans lined with paper baking cups and sprinkle with oats. Bake for 40 minutes.

Darlene's Favorite Dog Cookie

2 cups rye flour
1/2 cup vegetable oil
2/3 cup warm water
1/2 cup white flour
1/4 cup cornmeal

Mix well. I usually add about 1/4 tsp. either vanilla or mint flavor.
Roll out to 1/4" thick. Cut into shapes (I usually use about a 3-4" bone-shape cutter). Bake on lightly greased cookie sheet for 30 minutes at 350 degrees.

Divine Doggy Dinner

1/2 pound ground beef -- or turkey, chicken, lamb
1/4 cup cooked rice1 small potato
1/4 cup green beans -- about 5-8 beans
1/4 teaspoon garlic powder

Brown the meat in a pan. When completely cooked, drain the fat. Add the cooked rice; mix well. Set aside. Cut the potato and beans into small bite-sized pieces. Place in a pot with water; bring to a boil. Simmer until veggies are tender (about 15-20 minutes). Drain. Add the vegetables to the meat mixture. Add garlic powder; toss thoroughly under low heat. Let the dinner cool thoroughly before serving to prevent burning.

Yield: about 2 dinners

51

Dixie's Delights

1 ripe banana
1/2 cup peanut butter
1/4 cup wheat germ
1/4 cup unsalted peanuts -- chopped

In a small bowl, mash banana and peanut butter together using a fork. Mix in wheat germ. Place in refrigerator for about an hour until, firm. With your hands, roll rounded teaspoonfuls of mixture into balls. Roll balls in peanuts, coating them evenly. Place on cookie sheet in freezer. When completely frozen, pack into airtight containers and store in freezer.

Dog Mini Cakes

2 cups whole wheat flour
1/2 cup soybean flour
1 cup skim milk -- or water
1 tablespoon honey
1 tablespoon canola oil -- or sunflower
1 teaspoon sea salt

Mix dry ingredients. Add liquid and honey. Mix and let the dough rest in a warm place for 15 minutes. Add oil and allow to sit another 1/2 hour. Take walnut size portions of dough and flatten into small cakes. Bake in oven at 400 for 1/2 hour.

Dog Biscuits #1

2 1/2 cups whole wheat flour
1 teaspoon brown sugar
1/2 cup powdered milk
6 tablespoons butter
1/2 teaspoon salt
1 egg -- beaten
1/2 teaspoon garlic powder
1/2 cup ice water

Combine the flour, milk, salt, garlic powder and sugar. Cut in butter until mixture resembles cornmeal. Mix in egg; then add enough ice water to make a ball. Pat dough to 1/2" thick on a lightly oiled cookie sheet. Cut out shapes with a cookie cutter or biscuit cutter and bake on cookie sheet for 25 minutes at 350 degrees. Remove from the oven and cool on a wire rack.

To vary the flavor and texture, at the time the egg is added, add any of the following: 1 c. purred cooked green vegetables or carrots; 6 T. whole wheat or rye kernels; 3 T. liver powder. (The last two items are available in health food stores.)

Butter, margarine, shortening, or meat juices may be used.

Dog Biscuits #2

1 envelope dry yeast
1 cup rye flour
1/4 cup warm water
1/2 cup nonfat dry milk
1 pinch sugar
4 teaspoons kelp powder
3 1/2 cups all-purpose flour
4 cups beef or chicken broth
2 cups whole wheat flour
2 cups cracked wheat or 1 c. cornmeal

GLAZE: 1 large egg 2 tablespoons milk

Place 2 oven racks in the upper and lower thirds of the oven. Preheat oven to 300 degrees. Sprinkle the dry yeast or crumble the compressed yeast over the water. Add the pinch of sugar and allow yeast to sit in a draft-free spot for 10 - 20 minutes.

The mixture should be full of bubbles. If not, the yeast is too old to be useful. Stir well to dissolve the yeast. In a large bowl, place all the dry ingredients and stir well to blend them. Add the yeast mixture and 3 cups broth.

Using your hands, in the bowl, mix to form the dough adding more broth if needed to make the dough smooth and supple. Half a batch at a time, knead the dough briefly on a lightly floured counter. (Keep the second batch of dough covered with a moist towel while shaping and cutting the first.)

Roll out the dough into 18 x 13 x 1/4" rectangle. Cut into desired shapes using 3 1/2" one cutter or 2 1/2" cookie cutter. Re-roll the scraps. Repeat procedure with remaining dough.

For an attractive shine, lightly beat together the egg and the milk.
Brush the glaze on the cookies. Bake for 45 - 60 min. or until brown and firm. For even baking, rotate the cookie sheets from top to bottom 3/4 of the way thru the baking period. Use a small, angled metal spatula to transfer the cookie to wire racks to cool completely before using for the next batch.

Dog Biscuits #3

3 1/2 cups flour
4 teaspoons salt
2 cups whole wheat flour
1/2 cup dry milk
1 cup rye flour
1 egg
1 cup cornmeal
1 package dry yeast (1 T.)
2 cups cracked wheat
1 pint chicken stock

(Ingredients not generally available at grocery stores may be found at health food stores.)

Dissolve yeast in 1/4 c. warm water. Add chicken stock and pour into dry ingredients. Knead for 3 minutes, working into a stiff dough. Roll dough into a 1/4" thick sheet and cut with cookie cutters (cutters shaped like dog biscuits are available). Bake in 300 degree oven for 45 min., then turn oven off and leave biscuits in oven overnight. In the morning the biscuits will be bone hard.

NOTE: This dough is extremely stiff to work with, but the end product is excellent!

Dog Biscuits #4

2 3/4 cups whole wheat flour
1/2 cup powdered milk
1 teaspoon salt
1/4 teaspoon garlic powder
1 egg
6 tablespoons vegetable oil
8 tablespoons water -- (8 to 10)
2 jars Babyfood, Meat, Beef, Strained -- *see Note

Mix all ingredients together and knead for 3 min. Roll out to
`/1 inch thick. Use a dog bone shaped cookie cutter, and
place biscuits on an ungreased baking sheet. Bake in preheated oven at 350 degrees for 20 to 25 min.

MAKES approx. 2 dozen doggie biscuits

Note: Strain. Use beef, chicken or lamb

Dog Biscuits #5

1 cup whole wheat flour
1 cup white flour
1/2 cup powdered milk
1/2 cup wheat germ
1/2 teaspoon salt
6 tablespoons shortening
1 egg -- slightly beaten
1 teaspoon brown sugar
1/2 cup cold water

Stir dry ingredients well and then cut in the shortening. Stir egg and brown sugar into the flour mixture. Blend in water. Knead dough 10 to 12 strokes. Flour surface if dough sticks. Roll dough out to approximately 3/8 inches. Cut with a bone shaped cookie cutter.

Bake at 325 degrees for 30 minutes or until dough is firm to the touch.

Makes about 40.

Dog Biscuits For Your Favorite Dog

2 cups whole wheat flour
1 cup cornmeal
2/3 cup Brewer's yeast
2 teaspoons garlic powder
1/2 teaspoon salt
2 egg yolks
3 beef bouillon -- or chicken
1/2 cup boiling water

Preheat oven to 375 degrees.

Mix well. Working with half the dough at a time, roll dough to 3/8 inch thickness. Cut into desired shapes.

Bake for 20 minutes on ungreased cookie sheet. Turn oven off but leave biscuits in oven until crunchy.

Makes about 1 pound of dog biscuits that you dog is sure to love

Dog Bones

2 1/4 cups whole wheat flour
1/2 cup nonfat dry milk
1 egg
1/2 cup vegetable oil
1 beef bouillon cube
1/2 cup hot water
1 Tablespoon brown sugar

Preheat the oven to 300 degrees.

In a large mixing bowl, combine all ingredients, stirring until well blended. Knead dough 2 minutes.

On a floured surface, use a floured rolling pin to roll out dough to 1/4-inch thickness. Using a bone shaped cookie cutter cut out bones.
Bake 30 minutes on an ungreased baking sheet. Remove from pan and cool on wire rack.

Dog Cookies

1 c Beef, chicken, or vegetable stock
1 c Bread or all-purpose flour
1 c Whole wheat or rye (or other-dark) flour
1 c Bulgur wheat
1/4 c Non-fat dry milk powder
1/2 ts Salt
1 1/2 ts Yeast

Use dough cycle. Roll dough to 1/4" thickness. Cut with cookie cutters or knife. Place on baking sheets sprinkled with cornmeal. Cover with clean kitchen towels and let rise in warm place about 45 minutes. Bake at 325-degrees for 45 minutes. When all are baked, turn off oven and return all cookies to cooling oven overnight to harden. Store in airtight container.

(Using a 3.5" bone shaped cutter, you'll get about 30-35 cookies from this recipe.)

Dog Cookies With Chicken Broth

2 cups whole wheat flour
2/3 cup yellow cornmeal
1/2 cup sunflower seeds -- shelled
2 tablespoons corn oil
1/2 cup chicken broth
2 eggs
1/4 cup low-fat milk
1 egg -- beaten

Heat oven to 350 degrees. In a large bowl, mix together flour, cornmeal and seeds. Add oil, broth and egg mixture. The dough should be firm. Let sit 15-20 minutes. On a lightly floured surface, roll out dough 1/4 inch thick. Cut into shapes and brush with beaten egg. Bake for 25-35 minutes, until golden brown. Remove and cool. Store in airtight container.

Dog Oil Supplement

1/4 cup olive oil
1/4 cup canola oil
1/4 cup cod liver oil
1/4 cup flax seed oil

Place oils in brown bottle and shake well. Store in refrigerator.
Add two teaspoons to the dogs food each day. Can be add to dry food as well.

Safflower and Sunflower oil may used as well.

Dog Pooch Munchies

3 cups Whole wheat flour
1 teaspoon Garlic salt
1/2 cup Soft bacon fat
1 cup Shredded cheese
1 Egg -- beaten slightly
1 cup Milk

1. Preheat oven to 400 F. degrees.

2. Place flour and garlic salt in a large bowl. Stir in bacon fat. Add cheese and egg. Gradually add enough milk to form a dough. Knead dough and roll out to about 1 inch thick.

3.Use dog bone cookie cutter to cut out dough. Place on greased cookie sheet. Bake about 12 minutes, until they start to brown. Cool and serve.

Dog Powder Mix

1 cup brewer's yeast
1 cup bone meal
1/2 cup kelp powder
1/2 cup alfalfa powder

Mix well add to air-tight container. Keep in freezer if desired add one tablespoon to dogs food each day.

Doggie Biscuits

3/4 c Hot water or meat juice
1/3 c Margarine
1/2 c Powdered milk
1/2 ts Salt
1 Egg, beaten
3 c Whole wheat flour

Mix well - roll in to small logs in your hands and bake at 325 degrees for about 50 mins.

Doggie Bone Treats

1 cup all-purpose flour
1 cup whole wheat flour
1/2 cup wheat germ
1/2 cup nonfat dry milk
3 tablespoons vegetable shortening
1 teaspoon brown sugar
1/2 teaspoon salt
1 egg
1/3 cup water

Preheat the oven to 350 degrees.

Coat a cookie sheet with nonstick cooking spray. In a large bowl, combine both flours, wheat germ, nonfat dry milk, shortening, brown sugar, and salt; mix until crumbly. Add the egg and water; mix well.
On a lightly floured surface, knead the dough until smooth. Using a rolling pin, roll out to a 1/2-inch thickness. Using a dog bone-shaped cookie cutter or a knife, cut out biscuits. Place on the cookie sheet and bake for 25 to 30 minutes, or until lightly browned.

Remove to a wire rack to cool completely. Of course, beware of any of your dog's possible allergies to wheat, eggs, or dairy products.

Doggie Quiche

4 whole egg
1 tablespoon cream
2/3 cup milk, skim
3 ounces meat -- *see Note
2 ounces shredded low fat cheddar cheese -- or other type
1 whole pie crust (9 inch)
1/2 teaspoon garlic powder -- optional
1 sprig parsley -- chopped fine

Pre-heat oven to 375F degrees.

Wisk egg, cream, milk together, then pour into pie crust. Add meat, cheese evenly Bake for 30-45 min. Till done. Let it cool. Sprinkle fresh parsley.

Note: fine chopped, any type of meat they like. Pre cooked, unless you use liver.

Fresh shredded veggies can be used as well.

Doggy Biscuits

1 package dry yeast
1/4 cup warm water
2 cups beef broth -- at room temperature
1/4 cup milk
1/2 cup honey
1 egg -- beaten
1/4 cup margarine
1 teaspoon salt
2 1/2 cups flour
1 cup cornmeal
1 cup wheat germ
2 cups cracked wheat
3/4 cup wheat bran
3/4 cup oatmeal
3/4 cup grated cheddar cheese
3 cups whole wheat flour

TOPPING
1 cup beef broth
1/2 teaspoon garlic powder
3 tablespoons oil

In a small bowl, dissolve yeast in warm water. In a large bowl, combine beef broth, milk, honey, egg, bacon grease or margarine, and salt.

Add yeast/water mixture and mix well. Stir in flour, corn meal, wheat germ, cracked wheat, wheat bran, oatmeal, and cheese.

Add whole wheat flour, 1/2 cup at a time, mixing well after each addition.

Knead in the final amounts of flour by hand to make a stiff dough.

Continue to knead for 4 to 5 minutes.

Pat or roll to 1/2 inch thickness.

Cut into bone shapes and place on a greased baking sheet.

Cover lightly and let set (rise) for 30 minutes

Doggy Dip

3 tablespoons peanut butter
2 tablespoons honey
1 banana -- *See Note
16 ounces vanilla yogurt
1 tablespoon whole wheat flour

Mix the peanut butter, honey, and fruit together until well blended. In a separate bowl, combine the yogurt and flour, mix well. Add the fruit mixture to the yogurt and blend together. Keep cold in refrigerator.
Use this dip to coat or dip biscuits and treats into. Allow treats to chill in refrigerator until coating is set and firm; this prevents big messes!

Note: Very Ripe, or a large jar of baby food fruit, any flavor

Ellie's Dog Biscuits

1 cup bran
1 1/2 cups whole meal flour
1/2 cup olive oil -- sunflower or SoyaOlive is great for their coat
1/2 cup sunflower seeds
1 cup oatmeal
1 egg
1 cup milk or water
1 teaspoon brewers yeast
1/2 teaspoon salt or kelp
1/2 cup coconut
1 comfrey leaf -- finely chopped. -- (can add parsley etc.)

Mix everything together and form balls (or shapes!) with your hands.
Place on baking tray and flatten with a fork. Bake slowly at 150 degrees C until hard - about 40 - 45 minutes. I double the recipe and it makes heaps - about 2 trays.

Ellie's Dog Loaf

2 1/8 cups water
2 cups brown rice
2 large potatoes
2 large carrots
1 1/8 pounds pumpkin
1 large onion
2 cloves garlic
3/4 bunch silver beet
1 cup whole meal pasta -- or Soya pasta
2 cups rolled oats
1 cup whole meal flour
1 1/8 pounds mince (or liver or fish)
3 eggs

Boil the rice in water for 10 - 15 minutes and chop the veggies (I put them through the food processor) Add the veggies and pasta to the rice and cook for 10 minutes. Turn off the heat and leave to cool (not vital if you're like me and in a rush!) Add mince, eggs, herbs, rolled oats and flour and mix together. Add more oats or flour if mixture is sticky (should be like a fruit cake mix)

Spoon into oiled and floured loaf tins and bake in a hot oven 180 degrees CENTIGRADE for 1 hour.

Remove from tins ,turn oven off and return loaves to oven for 5 - 10 minutes to firm bottom crust.

Take out of oven, leave to cool and use immediately or wrap in foil and freeze. Makes about 3 - 4 loaves.

Fido's Cheese Nuggets

1 cup Oatmeal -- uncooked
1 1/2 cups Hot Water -- or Meat Juices
4 oz Grated Cheese -- one cup
1 Egg -- beaten
1 cup Wheat Germ
1/4 cup Margarine
1/2 cup Powdered Milk
1/4 teaspoon Salt
1 cup Cornmeal
3 cups Whole Wheat Flour

In large bowl pour hot water over oatmeal and margarine: let stand for 5 minutes. Stir in powdered milk, grated cheese, salt and egg. Add cornmeal and wheat germ. Mix well. Add flour, 1/3 cup at a time, mixing well after each addition. Knead 3 or 4 minutes, adding more flour if necessary to make a very stiff dough. Pat or roll dough to 1/2 inch thickness. Cut into bone shaped biscuits and place on a greased baking sheet. Bake for 1 hour at 300 degrees. Turn off heat and leave in oven for 1 1/2 hours or longer.

Makes approximately 2 1/4 pounds.

Fido's Favorite Treats

1 cup oatmeal
1/3 cup butter
1 teaspoon beef bouillon granules
1/2 cup hot water
3/4 cup powdered milk
3/4 cup cornmeal
1 egg -- beaten
3 cups whole wheat flour

Combine oatmeal, butter, and bouillon granules in a large bowl. Pour hot water over this and let stand for 5 minutes. Stir in powdered milk, cornmeal, and egg. Add flour 1/2 c. at a time, mixing well after each addition. Knead for 3-4 minutes, adding more flour if needed to make a very stiff dough. Pat or roll out dough to 1/2" thickness, then cut into bone shaped pieces. Place in a greased baking sheet. Bake at 325* for 50 minutes. Allow to cool and dry out till hard.

Frozen Peanut Butter Yogurt Treats

32 ounces vanilla yogurt
1 cup peanut butter

1. Put the peanut butter in a microwave safe dish and microwave until melted.

2. Mix the yogurt and the melted peanut butter in a bowl.

3. Pour mixture into cupcake papers and freeze.

Fruity Yogurt Treats

2 kiwi fruit -- mashed, or jar baby food fruit
8 ounces strawberry yogurt -- or other

Mix together, freeze in ice cube tray. serve.

Gingham Dog and Cat Biscuits

1 cup whole wheat flour
2 tablespoons wheat germ
1/4 cup bran flakes
1/4 cup soy flour
1 tablespoon molasses
2 tablespoons oil -- or fat
1 tablespoon kelp -- or salt
1 teaspoon sage
1/2 teaspoon bone meal1/3 cup milk -- or water

Mix all ingredients together. Knead and shape into crescents, rounds or sticks for dogs. For cats, roll out and cut into narrow strips or ribbons. Bake 25-30 minutes in a moderate oven (350 degrees) until lightly toasted. Watch the narrow strips as they tend to get done sooner than the others. If the biscuits are not hard enough, leave them in the oven with the heat turned off for an hour or as long as desired.

Glazed Beagle Biscuits

2 teaspoons beef bouillon granules
1/3 cup Canola Oil
1 cup boiling water
2 cups rolled oats
3/4 cup cornmeal
1/2 cup milk
1 cup grated cheese
1 egg -- beaten
1 cup rye flour
2 cups white flour

Add bouillon and oil to boiling water then add oats. Let mixture stand for a few minutes. Stir in the cornmeal, milk, cheese, and egg. Slowly stir in the flours. Knead on a lightly floured surface until the dough is smooth and no longer sticky. Roll out to about 1/4 inch thick and cut into bone shapes. Place on a greased baking sheet. Spoon topping over biscuits. Turn them over and repeat with other side. Bake at 325 for 45 minutes or until lightly browned on bottom. Turn off the oven and leave biscuits in until cool.

Good for You Gobblers

1 cup white flour
1 cup whole wheat flour
1/4 cup sunflower seeds -- chopped
2 tablespoons applesauce
1 tablespoon peanut butter
1/4 cup molasses
2 eggs -- beaten
1/4 cup milk

Mix the dry ingredients (flour and seeds) together. Add applesauce, peanut butter and molasses and stir well. In a separate bowl mix the egg and milk together. Add to the dough. Add a little more milk if the mixture is too dry - you want a firm dough. Knead for a few minutes. Roll out to 1/2" thickness. Cut into desired shapes. Bakes at 350 degrees for 30 minutes, or until biscuits are brown and firm.

Goulash

1 pound ground beef -- *see Note
2 cups cooked brown rice
2 cans vegetables -- *see Note
2 whole eggs -- *see Note
1 can mackerel, canned
2 cloves garlic -- minced
1 pound chicken liver -- or gizzards

Pulverize veggies, either in a blender, processor, grinder, etc. Mix all ingredients together in a big pot. Add enough water to cover, mix well. if you feed raw, which we do, place into containers, enough for one feeding in each, and freeze. We use plastic baggies. If you don't feed raw, cover the pot and simmer for about 2 hrs, stirring occasionally. When it is done cooking, cool, and place into containers or baggies, enough for one feeding in each and freeze. Simply get out in the morning to thaw in the fridge.

Note: ground beef, ground turkey, ground venison, etc.

Note: fresh veggies (about 3 cups)- broccoli, asparagus, sweet potatoes, green beans, carrots, spinach, kale. CUT UP.

Note: shells crushed and added Dogs get this every evening for dinner, with 1/4-1/2c kibble mixed in, depending on size of dog. feed 1cup per 15 lbs body weight.

Greyhound Green Bean Grub

1 pound green beans -- fresh or frozen, sliced
1 can cream of mushroom soup
1/2 cup milk
1/2 cup cheddar cheese -- plus extra

Mix all ingredients together except beans. Place beans in oven casserole, add sauce mixture and stir well. Cover and bake in a 350 degree oven for 25 minutes. Uncover the casserole and sprinkle top with more cheddar cheese. Bake 5 minutes more. Let cool.

Healthy Snacks

1 cup white rice flour
1/4 cup soy flour
1/4 cup egg substitute
1 tablespoon molasses -- unsulphered
1/3 cup milk
1/3 cup powdered milk
2 tablespoons safflower oil

Preheat oven to 350 degrees. Mix dry ingredients together. Add molasses, egg, oil and milk. Roll out flat onto oiled cookie sheet and cut into dally bite-sized pieces. Bake for 20 minutes. Let cool and store in tightly sealed container.

Home Made Dog Biscuits

1 package active dry yeast
1 cup warm chicken broth
2 tablespoons molasses
1 3/4 cups all purpose flour -- (1 3/4 to 2)
1 1/2 cups whole wheat flour
1 1/2 cups cracked wheat
1/2 cup cornmeal
1/2 cup non fat dry milk powder
2 teaspoons garlic powder
2 teaspoons salt1 tablespoon milk
1 egg -- beaten

Dissolve yeast in 1/4 cup warm water, 110 to 115 degrees. Stir in broth and molasses. Add 1 cup only of the all purpose flour, all the whole wheat flour, cracked wheat, cornmeal, dry milk, garlic salt and mix well. On floured board, knead in remaining flour. Roll out 1/2 at a time to 3/8" thick. Cut in desired shapes. Place on ungreased baking sheet, brush tops with beaten egg and milk mixture. Repeat remaining dough. Bake at 300 degrees for 45 minutes. Turn oven off and let dry overnight.

Makes 42 to 48.

Home Made Party Cake

2/3 cup ripe mashed bananas
1/2 cup softened butter
3 large eggs
3/4 cup water
2 cups Unbleached Flour
2 teaspoons baking powder
1 teaspoon baking soda
2 teaspoons cinnamon
1/2 cup chopped pecans
1/2 cup raisins

Frosting:

2 cup mashed banana
1 tablespoon butter
6 tablespoon carob flour
2 teaspoons vanilla
3 tablespoon unbleached flour
1 teaspoon cinnamon

Cake: In mixing bowl, beat together mashed banana and butter until creamy. Add eggs and water. Beat well. Stir in dry ingredients. Beat until smooth. Add nuts and raisins. Spoon batter evenly into oiled and floured bundt pan. Bake at 350 degrees for about 35 minutes. Cool on wire rack 5 minutes, remove from pan, replace on rack and cool.

Frosting: Blend thoroughly and spread on cool cake. Sprinkle with chopped pecans. The frosting contains carob, which is a safe (almost tastes like) chocolate substitute.

Homemade Liver Treats

1 cup whole wheat flour
1 cup cornmeal
1/2 cup wheat germ
1 teaspoon garlic powder
1 pound beef liver

Pre-heat oven to 350.

Liquefy liver in blender, add dry ingredients. Grease cookie
sheet. Drop teaspoonfuls of mixture onto cookie sheet and
flatten with bottom of glass dipped in water and cornmeal.
Bake for 15-20 minutes.

You may store baked or unbaked dough in freezer.

Hors D'ogs

1/4 cup cheddar cheese -- grated
2 tablespoons safflower oil
1/2 cup rice krispies®
1/2 teaspoon minced garlic
1/4 cup swiss cheese -- grated

Combine cheeses, garlic and oil. Using plastic wrap, shape mixture into a log about 1 inch in diameter and 8 inches long. Roll log in Rice Krispies. Refrigerate. Slice into half-inch rounds and serve.

Icy Paws

2 cartons plain or vanilla yogurt (32 oz each)
1 small can tuna in water (8oz.)
2 tsp. garlic power
24 3 oz. plastic cups (not paper)

Open yogurt, if they are full to the top use a spoon & scoop out one cup.(these will be frozen as plain yogurt). Put half of the can of tuna in each yogurt container add the garlic power (1 tsp. in each) & stir thoroughly.

Use a spoon & scoop the mixture into the cups. Place on a tray & freeze overnight.

Makes about 24 treats.

VARIATIONS: Mix in garlic powder, brewers yeast & fennel seed. Veggie Delight: Mix in cooked peas or other vegetables. Chicken Icy Paws: use canned chicken instead of tuna Potassium Boost: Add in a mashed banana.

Jake's Dog Biscuits

2 1/2 cups whole wheat flour
1/2 cup powdered milk
1/2 teaspoon garlic powder
1/2 teaspoon salt
1 teaspoon brown sugar
6 tablespoons margarine -- or shortening
1 egg -- beaten
3 tablespoons liver powder
1/2 cup ice water

Preheat oven to 350 degrees. In a large bowl, combine flour, powdered milk, garlic powder, salt and sugar. Cut in margarine. Mix in egg, then add liver powder. Add ice water until mixture forms a ball. Pat out dough 1/2" thick on a lightly oiled cookie sheet. Cut with any size cutter. Remove scrapes and redo. Bake 30 min.

Lab Liver-Chip Cookie

2 cups Whole wheat flour
1/3 cup Butter -- melted
1 Egg -- beaten
6 tablespoons Water
1/4 cup liver -- dried or jerky-style treats -- chopped

Preheat oven to 350 degrees. Combine flour, butter, egg, and water. Mix well. Blend in liver bits. Turn onto a greased baking pan. Bake 20 to 25 minutes. Cool and cut.

Labrador Loaf

1 cup Amaranth
1 cup Dates -- dried
1 cup boiling water -- or beef broth
2 cups whole wheat flour
2 teaspoons baking powder -- non aluminum sulfate
2 tablespoons canola oil
4 ounces Egg Beaters ® 99% egg substitute
2 cups beef broth
1/2 pound ground beef, extra lean

Put Amaranth and Dates in a bowl, pour boiling water over and allow to soak 30 minutes. Pre-heat oven to 350.

In a large bowl, mix egg beaters and canola oil and beef broth and beef, mix well. Add whole wheat flour and baking soda, and the soaked Amaranth and Dates. Mix well.

Pour into an oiled loaf pan, bake for 1 hour or till done.

*Note: Use Vegetable Broth and 1/2 Pound of Textured Vegetable Protein for a Vegetarian Diet

Lhasa Apso Lamb

1 pound lamb, ground -- cooked
2 cups cooked brown rice
2 cups cooked white rice1 cup yogurt, skim milk
4 cloves garlic -- crushed
1/4 cup green beans, frozen -- chopped
1/4 cup carrots, frozen -- chopped
1/4 cup kale, frozen -- chopped

Cook Lamb and drain off excess fat if desired. Defrost frozen veggies, but don't cook them and chop to desired size.

In a large bowl mix cooked lamb, cooked rice, chopped vegetables, garlic and yogurt.

Slightly heat if desired to serve.

Refrigerate or freeze portions in zip lock bags. Should yield 3 to 6 servings.

Liver Brownies

1lb. chicken or beef liver
½ lb. PLAIN cornmeal (non rising)
½ lb. plain old-fashioned oatmeal
1 can salmon or mackerel (with juice)
1 Cup chicken broth or water
1 Tablespoon minced garlic
1 egg
Dash of salt
¼ Cup parsley flakes

Place liver, egg, fish, broth, garlic, salt and parsley flakes in a blender or food processor and blend until smooth. Mix corn and oatmeal's, and then add liver mixture. Mix well. Once mixed, batter should be like a slightly wet brownie mix. Add more broth or water if necessary. Pour mixture onto well-greased cookie sheet and bake at 250 degrees for 1 ½ to 2 hours. Cut into squares while still warm. Cool, and then freeze what you won't use in 1 week or less.

Liver Treats

1 pound beef liver

All you need are beef livers. Try your local meat packers; they often throw them away. Or you can buy fresh liver from the supermarket. Cut the liver into approximately 1 inch slices.

Place in your food dehydrator for 24 hours*. Use Pam or the equivalent on the drying racks, so the liver won't stick. Let dry for 24 hours.

*Or you could place them on a cookie sheet and bake in a 325 degree oven for about 45 minutes to help dry them out.

Liver Treats For Dogs

1 pound beef liver
2 garlic cloves
1 Box corn muffin mix

Preheat oven to temperature in corn muffin directions.

Mix liver and garlic in a blender or food processor, then process till liquid. Stir in muffin mix, then scrape onto a baking sheet and pat to app. 1/2-1" thickness. Bake till very firm, but not burned.

Cut into squares, then store in refrigerator or freezer.

Lucy's Liver Slivers

1/2 pound chicken livers -- cooked
1 cup chicken stock
1/2 cup corn oil
1 tablespoon chopped parsley
1 cup powdered milk
1 cup rolled oats
1/2 cup brewer's yeast
1 cup soy flour
1 cup cornmeal
3 cups whole wheat flour

Preheat oven to 350°. In food processor or blender, process chicken livers, chicken stock, corn oil and parsley until smooth. Transfer to large bowl. Add powdered milk, rolled oats, brewer's yeast, soy flour and cornmeal. Mix well. Gradually add whole wheat flour. You'll have to use your hands here, kneading in as much of the flour as it takes to create a very stiff dough.

Roll dough out to 1/4" thick and cut into stick shapes, about 1/2" by 4" (depending on the size of your dog). A pizza cutter works great! Bake on ungreased cookie sheet for 20 to 25 minutes until lightly browned and crisp. Turn off heat and let biscuits dry out in oven for several hours. Store in the refrigerator.

Massive Mastiff Munchy Muffins

2 carrots
2 3/4 cups water
1 egg
1/4 teaspoon vanilla extract
2 tablespoons honey
1 1/2 banana -- *see Note
4 cups whole wheat flour
1 tablespoon baking powder
1 tablespoon cinnamon
1 tablespoon nutmeg

Shred the carrot with a hand shredder or in a blender. Mix all wet ingredients together in a bowl, then add the pureed banana. Mix together thoroughly. Set aside. Combine the dry ingredients. Add the wet ingredients to the dry and mix thoroughly, leaving no dry mixture on the bottom. Coat a 12 muffin pan with nonstick spray. Fill each muffin hole 3/4 full. Bake about 1 hour at 350 degrees.

Note: over ripe. Try replacing the banana with one apple for a different flavor!

Meat and Grain Menu

2 cups brown rice -- cooked
2/3 cup meat -- lean
2 teaspoons lard -- or veggie oil
1/4 cup Vegetables -- grated, no onion
*Supplements

Mix the above. You can cook the meat if you want to, use your judgment.

Serve slightly warm.

*For supplements, add 2 tsp. powder and 1 tsp. oil to feed daily- this is for a 5-15 lb. dog, use double supplements for a puppy.

Meatball Mania

1/2 pound ground beef
2 tablespoons grated cheese
1 carrot -- finely grated
1/2 teaspoon garlic powder
1/2 cup bread crumbs -- w/w is best
1 egg -- beaten
1/2 tablespoon tomato paste

Preheat oven to 350 degrees. Combine all ingredients together; mix thoroughly. Roll into meatballs - whatever size is appropriate for your dog.

Place on a cookie sheet sprayed with non-fat cooking spray. Bake for 15-20 minutes, or until they are brown and firm.

Cool and store in the fridge or freezer.

Munchie Crunchy Meat Treats

1/2 cup powdered milk -- non-fat
1 egg -- beaten
1 1/2 cups rice flour
1/2 teaspoon honey
1/2 cup water
5 teaspoons chicken broth -- or beef
1 jar baby food, meat, beef, strained -- meat, any flavor

Combine all ingredients well. Form into a ball. Roll dough out on a floured surface. Cut out desired shapes. Bake in a 350 degree oven for 25-30 minutes. Let cool. The treats should be hard and crunchy.

MuttLoaf

1/2 cup amaranth -- *see Note
1 1/2 cups chicken broth
1 1/2 pounds ground chicken -- or turkey
1/2 cup cottage cheese
2 whole egg
1/2 cup oats, rolled (raw)
1/4 cup carrot -- finely chopped
1/4 cup spinach -- finely chopped
1/4 cup zucchini -- finely chopped
2 cloves garlic
1 tablespoon olive oil

Add amaranth and chicken broth to sauce pan and bring to a boil, reduce heat and simmer for 20 minutes. Set aside and let cool.

Preheat oven to 350.

In a large mixing bowl add meat, cottage cheese, veggies, and eggs. Mix thoroughly. Add wheat germ, cooled amaranth and olive oil mix well.

Add mixture to loaf pan, bake at 350 for 1 hour or until done.

Note: Amaranth can be found in a health food store, if not use barley. Barley will need 4 cups of broth and 50 minutes to cook.

Mutt's favorite rice n' hamburger

2 cups rice
1/2 pound hamburger meat
1 teaspoon vegetable oil
1 clove garlic
1/2 cup carrots or broccoli or spinach
4 cups water

Put all ingredients into a large pot, boil until done, then cool off and serve.

Muttzoh Balls

1 cup natural dry dog food
2 Eggs -- beaten lightly
1 teaspoon cod liver oil
1/3 cup Cold water
2 dashes garlic powder
1/2 cup cream of chicken soup, condensed

Grind dry dog food smooth in a food processor or blender. Lightly beat egg and add oil. Mix all moist ingredients together except soup. Add to dry ingredients. Form into 1/2" balls. In large pan, bring 1 quart water to boiling to which you have added 1/2 cup chicken soup or the 2 bouillon cubes. Drop balls into boiling water. Boil for 3 minutes. Remove from water, drain and cool. Refrigerate

Peanut Butter and Honey Dog Biscuits

3/4 cup flour
1 egg
1 Tablespoon Honey
1 teaspoon peanut butter
1/4 cup vegetable shortening
1 teaspoon baking soda
1/4 teaspoon salt
1/4 cup rolled oats
1/2 teaspoon vanilla

Heat honey and peanut butter until runny (about 20 seconds in the microwave. Mix ingredients together and drop by 1/2 teaspoonful onto cookie sheet and bake at 350 degrees Fahrenheit for 8 to 10 minutes. My dog is a Pug, and a half a biscuit is plenty for her. So if you have a bigger or smaller dog, adjust the biscuit size (and the cooking time).
This normally makes about 45 to 50 biscuits.

Peanut Butter Cookies

2 cups whole wheat flour
1 cup wheat germ
1 cup peanut butter
1 egg
1/4 cup vegetable oil
1/2 cup water
1/2 teaspoon salt

Preheat oven to 350 degrees F.

Combine flour wheat germ and salt in large bowl then mix in peanut butter, egg oil and water. Roll dough out onto a lightly floured surface till about 1/2 inch thick, then cut out the biscuits using a cookie cutter -- (or make squares). Put the biscuits onto an ungreased baking sheet. Bake 15 mins for the smaller sized cookies and up to 35 mins. for larger shaped ones.

Store in the fridge .

Peanut Butter Dog Biscuits

2 1/2 Cups Whole Wheat Flour
1/2 Cup Powdered Milk -- non-fat
1 1/2 Teaspoons Sugar
1 Teaspoon Salt
1 Whole Egg
8 Ounces Peanut Butter -- (1 jar)
1 Tablespoon Garlic Powder
1/2 Cup Cold Water

Mix above ingredients together, adding water after other ingredients are mixed. Knead for 3 to 5 minutes. Dough should form a ball. Roll to 1/2 inch thick and cut into doggie bone shapes. Bake on a lightly greased cookie sheet for 30 minutes at 350 degrees.

Peanut Butter & Oats Glazed Goodies

1 cup water
1 cup quick cooking oats
1/4 cup butter -- half stick
1/2 cup cornmeal
1 tablespoon sugar
1 teaspoon salt
1/2 cup milk
1/3 cup peanut butter
3 cups whole wheat flour

Boil water in a saucepan. Add oats and butter. Let oats soak for ten minutes. Stir in the cornmeal, sugar, salt, milk, peanut butter, and egg. Mix thoroughly. Add the flour, one cup at a time (you may not need the entire amount) until a stiff dough forms.

Knead dough on floured surface until smooth, about 3 minutes. Roll to 1/2" thickness. Place on a greased cookie sheet.

Glaze:

1 large egg
2 tbsp. milk

Mix well. Brush glaze on dough with a pastry brush. Bake in a pre-heated 325 degree oven for 35-45 minutes or until golden brown.
Cool completely.

Pet Party Mix

2 cups Cheerios®
2 cups Chex mix
2 teaspoons gravy, dry mix, brown
1/2 cup Bacos®
2 cups Shredded Wheat® -- spoon size
1/2 cup melted butter -- or margarine
1/2 cup American Cheese -- grated
1 pieces Beef Jerky -- dog treats (pupperoni, Jerky Treats, etc.)

1. Preheat oven to 275 .

2. Pour melted butter/margarine into a 33x23 cm baking pan. Stir in cheese, bacon bits, and gravy mix. Add cereal and stir until all pieces are coated.

3. Heat until crisp, approx. 45 min.

4. Let cool and store in tightly sealed container.

Pet Puffs

1 package Dry yeast
1/4 cup Warm water(110-115F.)
1 1/2 cups Whole wheat flour
1 cup All-Purpose flour
1 package Unflavored gelatin
1 cup Non-fat dry milk powder
1/4 cup Corn oil
1 Egg
1 Can pet food -- (6 to 8 oz)
1/4 cup Water

Dissolve yeast in 1/4 cup warm water. Mix dry ingredients. Add all ingredients together. (Dough will be very stiff; it may be necessary to mix with your hands.) Drop dough by level half-teaspoons onto ungreased cookie sheet. Bake in a pre-heated 300F. oven 25 minutes.

Pooch Peanut Butter Swirls

Dough #1

4 cups whole wheat flour
1/2 cup cornmeal
1 1/3 cups water
1/3 cup peanut butter
1 egg

Dough #2

4 cups whole wheat flour
2/3 cup cornmeal
1/2 cup banana -- mashed
1 egg
1 1/4 cups water
2 tablespoons vegetable oil
2 tablespoons molasses
2 tablespoons cinnamon

Combine all #1 ingredients and mix thoroughly. Knead on a lightly floured surface. Set aside. Combine all #2 ingredients and mix thoroughly. Knead on a lightly floured surface.

Roll each dough separately to a 1/8 inch thickness, into rectangles. Lightly brush a little water over the top of the light dough. Place the dark dough on top, then roll up like a jelly roll. Wrap the roll in plastic and chill in the freezer for one hour. Cut the roll into 1/4 inch slices. Place them on a cookie sheet sprayed with non-stick spray. Bake at 350 degrees for one hour.

Poochie Pint-Sized Carrot Treats

1/2 cup cheddar cheese -- shredded
1/4 cup margarine -- half stick
1 drop red food coloring -- or more if needed
1 drop yellow food coloring -- or more if needed
1 jar baby food carrots1 cup all-purpose flour
1/2 garlic powder
1/4 cup milk -- or more if needed

Melt cheese and margarine in a saucepan, stirring frequently.
Take off heat. Stir in food dye, to make orange color. Add
carrots, flour, and garlic powder. Stir until well blended. Add
enough milk to form into a ball. Transfer to a mixing bowl
and chill for one hour.

Roll dough on a lightly floured, flat surface to 1/4" thickness.
Place on a cookie sheet lightly sprayed with nonfat cooking
spray. Bake in a preheated 350 degree oven for 20 - 30
minutes, or until golden brown. Cool completely.

Poodle Pasta

3 1/2 cups whole wheat flour
8 ounces beef liver
3 whole egg
1 tablespoon olive oil
8 tablespoons butter -- optional

Puree beef liver in blender until smooth. Add eggs and blend for about a minute. Put flour in a large mixing bowl and make a well in the center of the flour. Pour liver and egg mixture into well along with olive oil. Mix well until thoroughly combined. Turn dough out on floured board and knead well for at least 5 minutes or until smooth and shiny. Wrap dough in plastic wrap and let dough rest in refrigerator for at least 1 hour, no longer than 2 days. When ready to make pasta, divide dough into 8 equal portions, approximately 4 oz. each.

Form into desired pasta shapes with hands or use pasta machine. Cook in rapidly boiling water until al dente. For thin noodles, approximately 10 minutes, for thicker noodles a few minutes longer. Drain noodles and toss with 1 tablespoon butter per serving, if desired. Instead of butter, try tossing noodles with 1 tablespoon olive oil, canola oil or other oil high in omega-3 and omega-6 fatty acids.

Yield: "2 pounds"

Potatoes Au Canine

3 cups boiled potatoes -- sliced
2 tablespoons vegetables -- grated
1/2 cup Creamed cottage cheese
1 tablespoon Nutritional Yeast
2 tablespoons Grated carrots
1/4 cup Whole milk
1/4 cup Grated cheese

Layer in a casserole dish the first 5 ingredients. Then pour the milk on top of all; sprinkle with cheese. Bake about 15 minutes at 350 until cheese melts and slightly browns. Serve cool.

Notes: As a potato substitute, you can use 3 cups of cooked oatmeal or 3 cups cooked brown rice.

Pumpkin-Patch Dog Biscuits

1 1/2 cups whole wheat flour
1 tablespoon brown sugar
1/2 teaspoon ground cinnamon
1/2 teaspoon ground nutmeg
4 tablespoons butter-flavored Crisco
1/2 cup pumpkin, canned
1 whole egg
1/2 cup buttermilk

Preheat oven to 400 degrees. Combine flour, cinnamon and nutmeg and cut in shortening. Beat egg with milk and pumpkin and combine with flour, mixing well. Stir until soft dough forms. Drop by tablespoons onto ungreased cookie sheet and bake for 12 to 15 minutes. Let cool and serve.

Puppy Formulas

Recipe #1
2/3 Cup Goat milk canned (or just regular canned milk)
1/3 Cup water or Pedialyte
1 teaspoon Karo Syrup
1 cgg yolk
1 teaspoon Dyne or pediatric vitamin

Strain a couple of times to make sure there is no albumin in the mixture, although it has been used successfully without egg at all.

Variation: 1 can of Condensed Milk rather than goat's milk (it may be too high in protein and put a strain on the puppy's kidneys 1 envelope of Knox unflavored gelatin in addition to other ingredients (helps keep stools solid).

Recipe #2
1 cup of canned Condensed milk or evaporated milk
4 ounces plain, full-fat yogurt
1 egg yolk
1 dropper full of baby vitamins
Mix well.

Ravioli Woofer Stuffing

3 tablespoons whole wheat flour
3/4 cup cottage cheese, 2% fat
2 eggs
1/2 cup cooked Atlantic salmon -- finely diced
2 tablespoons parsley sprig -- finely chopped

Prepare the Poodle Rice and Meat Dinner
1 cup meat -- *see Note
4 cups rice
1 cup vegetables -- *see Note
1 tablespoon vegetable oil
2 cloves garlic

Boil all ingredients together in a large pot. Be sure that pork is cooked all the way through. Cool food off and serve.

Note: choose one: hamburger, ground pork (cook all the way through), ground chicken, ground turkey, or liver

Note: choose one or more of these: sweet potato, regular potato, green beans, carrots, spinach

Try to substitute mackerel (a fish) for meat in some meals. I usually buy the canned stuff which has little bones in it. They can eat these bones. A little of the canned stuff goes a long way though--it has a lot of salt!

Rice Flour Dog Cookie

1 1/2 cups white rice flour
1 1/4 cups grated cheddar cheese
1/4 pound safflower oil -- margarine
1 clove garlic -- crushed

Grate the cheese and let stand until it reaches room temperature. Cream the cheese with the softened margarine, garlic, and flour. Add enough milk to form into a ball. Chill for 1/2 hour. Roll onto floured board. Cut into shapes and bake at 375 for 15 minutes or until slightly brown, and firm. Makes 2 to 3 dozen, depending on size.

115 Rover's Reward

1 package active dry yeast
1 teaspoon sugar
2 cups all-purpose flour
2 cups whole-wheat flour
2 cups cornmeal
2 cups oatmeal -- uncooked
1 cup fresh mint leaves -- chopped, loose packed
1 cup parsley sprigs -- chopped, loose packed
1/2 cup toasted wheat germ
1 can beef broth -- (13 3/4 to 14 1/2 ounces)3/4 cup milk

1. Preheat oven to 350 degrees F. In small bowl, combine yeast, sugar, and 1/4 cup warm water (105 degrees to 115 degrees F.). Let stand until yeast foams, about 5 minutes.

2. In very large bowl, combine all-purpose flour, whole-wheat flour, cornmeal, oats, mint, parsley, and wheat germ. With wooden spoon, stir in yeast mixture, broth, and milk until combined. With hands, knead dough in bowl until blended, about 1 minute.

3. Divide dough in half. Cover 1 piece with plastic wrap to prevent drying out. Place remaining piece of dough on lightly floured surface. With floured rolling pin, roll dough to 1/4-inch thickness. With large (about 5 inches) or small (about 2 inches) cookie cutter, such as bone* or mailman, cut out as many biscuits as possible, reserving trimmings. With spatula, transfer biscuits to large ungreased cookie sheet. Reroll trimmings and cut more biscuits. Repeat with remaining dough.

4. Bake small biscuits 30 minutes, bake large biscuits 40 minutes. Turn oven off; leave biscuits in oven 1 hour to dry out.

5. Remove biscuits from cookie sheet to wire rack. When cool, store at room temperature in tightly covered container up to 3 months.
Yields: about 4 dozen large biscuits or 24 dozen small biscuits Work

Salmon Treats

1 can salmon, canned, pink
1/2 cup chopped parsley
3 eggs -- shells included
1/2 cup sesame seeds -- ground in coffee grinder
1/2 cup flax seeds -- ground in coffee grinder
2 cups potato flour -- (2 to 3)

Put these ingredients into a food processor, mix VERY WELL. Pour potato flour through the opening while the motor is running. I can't tell you exactly how much, but I would guess about 2-3 cups. When the dough forms, like a pie crust, and rolls into a ball it is ready to take out. Dump this mess onto potato floured counter or board. Knead more flour into this and when it is a rolled out cookie consistency, it is ready to roll out into about 14 inch thick. I use a pizza cutter to roll our long strips and then cut crosswise to make small squares . If you want FANCY you may use a cookie cutter. Bake on cookie sheets, sprayed Pam or line the sheet with parchment paper. I put in as many as will fit. Usually two whole cookie sheets suffices. I bake this in a 375º oven for 20 min. Turn and rotate the cookie sheets and bake about 10 more minutes. You can make them as soft or as hard as you want.

Scrumptious Carob Bake

6 cups white rice flour
1/8 cup peanut oil
1/8 cup margarine -- safflower oil type
1 Tbsp brown sugar
4 ounces carob -- chips, melted
1 cup water
1/4 cup molasses
1/2 cup powdered milk

Mix dry ingredients in a large bowl. Add remaining ingredients and mix until blended. Dough will be stiff. Chill. Roll dough on a greased cookie pan and cut into shapes 1/2 inch thick. Bake at 300 for 1 hour.

Sheltie Scones

2 1/2 cups self-rising flour
1 cup beef liver -- chopped
1/2 cup water -- or beef stock
1/2 cup milk
2 tablespoons butter
1/4 teaspoon salt

(Chopped Liver: Just boil the liver until it is gray and a rubbery consistency. Or if you have a microwave, cook it on high for about 8 mins. Chop it up into small pieces and when cool put the pieces into a number of airtight bags and store in the fridge. Use liver pieces as treats when training)

Scones: Sift flour and salt into a bowl, rub in butter. Add chopped liver. Use a knife to stir in milk and enough water to mix to a sticky dough. Turn dough onto lightly floured surface, knead quickly and lightly until dough is smooth. Press dough out evenly to about 2 cm and cut into rounds. Place on prepared tray and bake in very hot over for 15 minutes.

Makes about 16-18.

Shih Tzu Sushi

1 can salmon, canned, pink -- reserve liquid
1 cup brown rice
2 cups water -- plus salmon liquid
1 whole egg, hard-boiled -- chopped
1/2 cup peas and carrots, frozen -- or more if desired
1 tablespoon fresh parsley -- chopped
2 tablespoons cod liver oil
1 package Nori Sheets -- *see Note

Drain salmon, reserve liquid for rice. do not remove bones or skin, flake with fork. Defrost peas and carrots.

In a sauce pan add salmon liquid, water, brown rice, cook. let cool to touch.

In a mixing bowl add salmon, brown rice, chopped egg, peas and carrots, and parsley, cod liver oil. Mix well.

Place one nori sheet on a flat surface and spread mixture 1/4 inch over nori, leave 1/4 inch edge of nori and dampen with water. And roll, repeat till nori sheets are used, or mixture is gone.

Individually wrap in plastic wrap, refrigerate till ready to serve. Cut rolls into size for your dog.

Note: Nori Sheets is dried seaweed found in the oriental section of your grocery store or specialty shop. This recipe freezes well also.

Snickerpoodles Dog Treats

1/2 cup vegetable oil
1/2 cup shortening
1 cup honey
2 eggs
3 3/4 cups white flour
2 teaspoons cream of tartar
1 teaspoon baking soda
1/2 cup cornmeal
2 teaspoons cinnamon

Mix vegetable oil, shortening and honey together until smooth. Add eggs and beat well. Blend in flour, baking soda and cream of tartar. Knead dough until mixed well. Shape dough by rounded teaspoons into balls. Mix the cornmeal and cinnamon together in a bowl and roll balls in mixture. Place 2 inches apart on a cookie sheet that has been sprayed with a nonstick spray. Press the balls down with a fork twice going in 2 different directions or press with your favorite stamp. Bake 8 minutes at 400. Remove from baking sheet and cool on a rack.
Pasta recipe. form into the desired ravioli shape and size. Cover with damp cloth and set aside.

In a bowl, mix yogurt, whole wheat flour and eggs. Add salmon and parsley mix a few more moments.

Depending on ravioli size, place 1 to 4 teaspoons in center of each, moisten edges and fold.

Ravioli can be boiled or baked. If boiling, place in rapid boiling water for 10 to 15 minutes or till done. If baking pre-heat oven to 375, place ravioli on a baking sheet, put in oven for 20 to 25 minutes.

Note: use leftover meat such as beef, chicken, lamb etc. Also shredded veggies like carrots, sweet potato, etc. or chopped veggies such as green beans, broccoli, kale etc. raw oat meal and cooked rice or cooked barley, can be used in place of meat.

Surprise Snacks

1/4 cup hot water
8 chicken bouillon cube -- or beef
1 package dry yeast
1 1/2 cups tomato juice
2 cups flour -- divided
2 cups wheat germ
1 1/2 cups whole wheat flour

Place the hot water and bouillon cubes in a large mixing bowl and mash with a fork. Sprinkle yeast over this mixture and let stand about 5 minutes, until yeast is dissolved. Add the tomato juice, half the flour and the wheat germ and stir to form a smooth batter. Gradually work in the remaining flour and the whole wheat flour with your hands.

Divide the dough into 4 balls. Roll each ball out on a floured board to about 1/4" thick. Cut into shapes and place on ungreased cookie sheets about an inch apart. Bake in a 325F. oven for 1 hour, then turn off the heat and let biscuits dry in oven for about 4 hours or overnight with the door propped open slightly. Store in airtight container.

Tempting Training Treats

2 1/3 cups flour -- all-purpose or whole wheat
1/4 cup olive oil
1/4 cup applesauce
1/2 cup grated cheese -- like parmesan
1 large egg
1 teaspoon garlic powder
1/4 cup powdered milk -- non-fat

Combine all ingredients in a large bowl; mix well; Roll the
dough out to size of a cookie sheet; Pat the dough onto a
lightly greased cookie sheet, bringing it to the edges. Using a
sharp knife or a pizza cutter, cut desired sizes into dough
(just score through). If you're using as training treats, cut
them into small pieces; Sprinkle a little extra cheese and
garlic powder if desired on dough for flavor. Bake in a 350
degree oven about 15 minutes until golden brown. Turn off
the oven and let cool for a few hours; They will keep harden-
ing the longer you leave them. Break them apart; store
tightly covered or in the freezer.

Tess' Tantalizing Treats

1 cup oatmeal -- quick
1/4 cup margarine
1 1/2 cups hot water
1/2 cup powdered milk
1 cup grated cheddar cheese -- or Swiss, Colby
1/4 teaspoon garlic powder
1 egg -- beaten
1 cup cornmeal
1 cup wheat germ
3 cups whole wheat flour
1 tablespoon beef bouillon -- or chicken

1.Preheat oven to 300°.

2.In large bowl pour hot water over oatmeal and margarine (cut-up melts faster); let stand 5 minutes. Stir in powdered milk, grated cheese, garlic powder, bouillon and egg. Add cornmeal and wheat germ. Mix well. Add flour, 1/2 cup at a time, mixing well after each addition. Knead 3-4 minutes, adding more flour if necessary to make very stiff dough. Pat or roll dough to 1/2 inch thickness.

3.Cut into bone shaped biscuits and place on a greased baking sheet. Bake for 1 hour. Turn off heat and leave in oven an additional 1 1/2 hours or longer.

Makes approximately 2 1/4 pounds.

Trail Dog Grub

2 Cups Amaranth -- Cooked
1 Cup Lentils, Cooked
1 Cup Vegetables -- *See Note
2 Tablespoons Cod Liver Oil
1 Pound Buffalo
1 Cup Beef Broth

Cut Buffalo meat to size for your dog, add to Stock Pot along with beef broth, vegetables and cod liver oil, cook 10 minutes. Add Water if more moisture is needed during cooking.

Add cooked amaranth, cooked lentils mix well. Allow to cool and serve.
*Note: Chopped to size for your dog, Assorted Veggies, carrot, kale, sweet potato, asparagus, zucchini etc.

Traildog Biscuits

1 1/2 cups flour
1 1/2 cups whole wheat flour
1 tsp. garlic powder
1 cup rye flour
1 egg -- beaten1 cup oats
1/2 cup vegetable oil
1 cup cornmeal
1 3/4 cups beef broth -- or chicken
1/4 cup liver powder -- available in health food stores

Preheat oven to 300F. Mix all dry ingredients in a large bowl. Add egg, oil, and beef broth. Mix the dough, adding enough additional flour to make a dough that can be rolled. On a floured surface, roll to 1/2" thickness, then cut into shapes or squares. Prick with a fork. Bake for 2 hours. Turn the oven off, and let biscuits stand in oven overnight to harden. Store in airtight container.

Turkey Treats

2 cups cooked turkey -- cut up
2 cloves garlic
4 teaspoons grated cheese
1 tablespoon parsley -- freshly chopped
2 egg
2 cups whole wheat flour
2 tablespoons brewer's yeast
2 tablespoons vegetable oil

Combine turkey, garlic, cheese, parsley and mix well. Beat the eggs in a bowl and pour over turkey mixture. Add the flour, yeast, and oil. Stir until thoroughly mixed and all ingredients are coated. Drop into small lumps onto ungreased cookie sheet. Cook in a 350 degree oven for about 20 minutes, until brown and firm. Store in refrigerator.

Vegetarian Dog Biscuits

2 1/2 cups flour
3/4 cup Powdered Milk
1/2 cup vegetable oil
2 tbs. brown sugar
3/4 cup Vegetable Broth
1/2 cup carrots -- optional
1 egg

Preheat oven to 300F. Mix all ingredients into a ball and roll out to about 1/4" thick. Cut with bone-shaped cookie cutter, or strips, or a cutter shape of your own choice. Place on un-greased cookie sheet and bake 30 minutes at 300F.

Veggie Bones

3 cups minced parsley
1/4 cup carrots -- shredded
1/4 cup shredded mozzarella cheese
2 tablespoons olive oil
2 3/4 cups all-purpose flour
2 tablespoons bran
2 teaspoons baking powder
1/2 cup water -- possibly more

Preheat oven to 350 F, rack on middle level. Lightly greased baking sheet.

Stir together parsley, carrots, cheese, and oil. Combine all the dry ingredients and add to the veggies. Gradually add 1/2 cup of water, mixing well. Make a moist, but not wet dough. If needed add a little more water. Knead for one minute.

Roll out dough to 1/2 inch thickness. Using cookie cutter, cut out the shapes and transfer them to a baking sheet. Reroll the scraps and continue until dough is all used up.

Bake for 20 to 30 minutes until biscuits have browned and hardened slightly. They will harden more as they cool. Store in an airtight container.

Veggie Vittles

1 egg -- beaten
1/3 cup applesauce
1 cup vegetables -- *see Note
1 cup cooked rice
1 tablespoon brewer's yeast

Mix all ingredients well. Drop by rounded teaspoonfuls onto a greased cookie sheet. Bake in a preheated 350 degree oven for about 12 minutes, or until lightly browned and firm. Cool. Store in the fridge, or freeze.

Note: mashed or grated small. Any desired veggies can be used, such as zucchini, peas, carrots, potatoes, etc...

Vizsla Stew

2 cups barley
1/2 cup wild rice
9 cups chicken broth
4 cups rabbits -- boned, *See Note
1/2 cup kale -- chopped fine
1/2 cup asparagus -- chopped fine
1/2 cup lima beans -- chopped fine
1/2 cup carrots -- chopped fine
1 cup potato -- chopped fine
4 cloves garlic -- chopped fine
1/3 cup canola oil
1 cup yogurt, skim milk

In a large pot, place the bones and chicken broth. Bring to a rapid boil.
Add the long cooking Wild Rice and Barley, reduce heat to a simmer and cover. After 20 minutes and the rabbit, cook another 30 minutes.
Wash and chop the vegetables, place in a mixing bowl, add canola oil and yogurt, mix.

Allow Barley and Wild Rice to cool. Remove bones. Drain liquid if needed. Pour into the mixing bowl and mix well.

Refrigerate or freeze leftovers in portions in separate containers.

*Note: 2 rabbits, 4 to 6 pounds, bone the rabbit and cube to the size for your dog. Add the bones to the chicken broth.

Wacky Wheat Treats

2 jars baby food, meat, beef, strained -- *see Note
1/2 cup nonfat dry milk
2 ounces wheat germ
1/3 cup water
1/2 cup flour
1 teaspoon garlic powder

Mix together well. Roll out dough on floured surface. Cut out witch hat patterns and place on lightly greased cookie sheet. Bake in a 325 degree oven until golden brown, about 30-35 minutes.

Note: chicken, lamb, beef, etc.. - you choose.

Weimaraner Walleye

3 pounds walleye pike fillets
2 ounces chicken livers -- diced fine
2 cups fish stock
3 cups cooked brown rice
1/4 cup cooked wild rice
1/4 cup kale, frozen
1/2 cup green beans, frozen
1/4 cup collard greens, frozen
1/4 cup corn, frozen
1/4 cup potatoes, frozen
1 tablespoon cod liver oil

Pre heat oven to 350.

In a baking dish add walleye fillets diced chicken livers, pour
in fish stock and cod liver oil, add frozen veggies, cover and
bake 20 to 30 minutes or till done.

In a large bowl add cooked rice, and the juices from the baking dish along with the cooked veggies, mix well. chunk the
walleye into a size for your dog and mix well, if needed chop
vegetables to a size for your dog.

Allow to cool and serve. freeze leftovers or keep in fridge
covered.

Wolf-Dog Biscuits

2 cups whole wheat flour
3/4 cup cornmeal
4 tablespoons vegetable oil
2 cups all-purpose flour
4 beef bouillon cubes
2 cups boiling water
10 tablespoons bacon bits -- optional garlic

Combine first 4 ingredients; mix well. Dissolve bouillon cubes in boiling water and add bouillon to flour mixture. Mix to make stiff dough. Roll onto a floured surface. Cut out shapes with cookie cutters (or a drinking glass turned upside down can be used). Bake in preheated 300 degree oven for 30 minutes. Let stand overnight to harden.

This is the basic recipe.

Variations: use clear gravies from turkey, roast beef, etc. In place of bouillon cubes or clear soups. Crisp sausage bits could be used in place of bacon. Different spices could also be used (Italian, parsley, thyme, etc.).

Yogurt Pups

16 ounces plain nonfat yogurt
3/4 cup water
1 tablespoon chicken bouillon granules

Dissolve bouillon in water, Combine water and yogurt in blender and blend thoroughly, Pour into small containers for freezing, cover and freeze.

32123296R00085

Printed in Great Britain
by Amazon